# Propaganda Techniques

## By

## Henry T. Conserva

ISBN: 1-4107-0495-5  (e-book)
ISBN: 1-4107-0496-3  (Paperback)

This book is printed on acid free paper.

1stBooks – rev. 01/04/03

# INTRODUCTION

Persuading people to accept our ideas and do what we want them to do is a basic universal human activity.

There are many ways to get ideas and wants across to others. One way is to use physical force or threats of violence to achieve goals. This book attempts to examine a more gentle method of persuasion, specifically the use of written or spoken techniques of propaganda.

Propaganda is organized persuasion and involves the dissemination of biased ideas and opinions, often through the use of lies, deceptions, distortions, exaggerations and censorship. It is the communication of a point of view, moral, amoral or immoral, with the ultimate goal of the recipient of the view voluntarily accepting the propagandist's view. Propaganda has been used by dictatorial governments bent on conquest. America has fought two world wars in the twentieth century. In addition to the exchange of bullets there was an exchange of propaganda. When words are used as weapons the truth usually is the first victim. Small wonder the word "propaganda" has a negative connotation today.

The oldest trick of the propagandist is to demonize and dehumanize the hated other or others and make the enemy a faceless object. Doing this makes it easier to hurt the opponent. In recent wars propagandists have tried to mobilize hatred against the enemy, preserve the friendship of allies, and enlist the cooperation of neutrals. A major goal was to demoralize the enemy. The principle of any-means-to-an-end resulted in the spread of false rumors, the making of gross exaggerations and the telling of outright lies.

The propagandist has often imposed censorship to increase the effectiveness of propaganda. The Roman Catholic Church had its index of forbidden literature until 1966 and Hitler's Germany had its book burning sessions. America prohibited the printing of comic strips in which the term "atomic bomb" appeared.

The any-means-to-an-end principle seems to characterize much commercial advertising, political campaign oratory as well as messages delivered by all sorts of organizations, political, religious, business and social.

In my opinion, educators should be the natural enemies of propagandists. I see the educator's role as that of teaching people how to think while the propagandist's role is to teach people what to think.

An extreme form of propaganda that usually goes beyond the use of just words is brainwashing. Brainwashing is a method of influencing people to change their beliefs and accept as true what they previously had considered false, or to consider false what they previously had thought was true. Isolation, sleep and food deprivation and other terrible practices are considered to be appropriate if they worked to further the goal of mind control.

This book features eighty-nine selected techniques used in the art of propaganda. I can't count the number of ways in which propagandists work their trade. New techniques are being developed as I write. These eighty techniques are ones that I have seen used in past years. Some of them are losing their former importance while others are becoming more popular. I've organized the techniques under seven broad labels:

1. Faulty Logic

2. Diversion and Evasion

3. Appealing to the Emotions

4. Using Falsehoods and Trickery

5. Playing on Human Behavioral Tendencies, Mental Capacities and Processes

6. Speaking or Writing Styles

7. Reason or Common Sense

In undertaking the writing of this book I have been guided by the principle that to be forewarned is to be forearmed. We are all exposed to millions of persuasive messages in the mass media. All signs point to the propaganda blitz continuing and probably increasing. We need to protect ourselves from the distortions of fact that daily assault us. We need to recognize what techniques are being used on us and we also need to be on the lookout for new ones designed to entrap either our minds or our wallets or both.

# TABLE OF CONTENTS

## SECTION 1 – TECHNIQUES OF FAULTY LOGIC

**SIMPLIFICATION**

It's faulty reasoning to imagine that the simplification of a complex idea, issue or problem can be done without sacrificing some content and understanding of the message. This being said, it is often necessary for a propagandist to simplify complexities in order to have even the skeleton of his or her ideas understood and accepted

Simplification can reach a broad audience for several reasons. Complex messages take time to fully comprehend and when people are rushed, they tend to ignore what is being said. Another reason for a propagandist to simplify some idea or issue is to reach an audience with poor language skills.

When a bank sponsors a commercial that states, "…all your troubles will be over when you take out a loan with us", simplification is at work.

A propagandist must be careful in using the simplification technique with a sophisticated audience that might feel that he or she was being condescending.

One way to easily simplify a message is to check the vocabulary being used. Foreign words or phrases, which might not be widely known, will be omitted and complex words will be replaced with simpler words more easily understood.

## CONCURRENCY

This is one of a group of illogical propaganda techniques still being widely used. Its form is usually stated in this way: A with B, therefore A cause of B. When a propagandist has a clearly defined goal he or she can often use concurrency to either support something wanted or attack something unwanted.

Let's say there is a builder of tract houses. The propagandist wants to present reasons to a town council in support of a proposed project. Using concurrency an attempt is made to make as many associations as possible between the proposed project and various positive factors or trends in the target community. If economic conditions are good in the area, the builder attempts to show a causal relationship between home construction and a booming economy. The builder will say that home construction and general prosperity walk hand in hand.

In another example of concurrency, let's say a propagandist is opposed to motion pictures with explicit sexual themes being shown where he or she lives. The propagandist begins to research what's going on in the community looking for negative data to support the position being advocated. Statistics on unwed mothers, abandoned newborn babies, sexual crimes such as rape or pederasty will be gathered. In trying to make causal connections between motion picture content and the negative data the propagandist has gathered, he or she will try to persuade others that censorship of such films is necessary.

## POST HOC

This technique follows the pattern that A precedes B, therefore A is the cause of B.

As an example let's imagine a hypothetical nation somewhere in the mid-Pacific Ocean. We can picture a place which is run by two political parties; party one and party two. An advocate of the party might claim that a great war occurred when party two was at the helm and would try to link that war with the foreign policy of party two. In fact, there might not be any provable relationship.

On the other hand, an advocate of party two might say that a great economic depression occurred while party one ran the nation and would try to link the economic depression with the economic policies of party one. Here also there might not be any provable relationship.

Any time a driven propagandist can associate something negative with someone or something he or she doesn't like, the temptation to use a post hoc argument is difficult to resist.

**GENERALIZATION**

A generalization can be identified as having the following form: A1 is B, A2 is B, A3 is B, therefore all As are B. An example would be that if you know an Italian professor who is intelligent, an Italian judge who is intelligent and an Italian doctor who is intelligent you might conclude that all Italians are intelligent. It may be said that this line of reasoning is ridiculous but generalizations such as the example given pass for reasoning every day in some circles.

Any time a propagandist says the words all, none or never, a listener or reader can suspect that an error is being made. It only takes one exception to disprove a generalization. If *most* is substituted for *all* there will still be the burden of proving that 50% + 1 of all Italians are intelligent.

3

A safer way out of these burdens is to say that *some* Italians are intelligent. Statements with the word some are usually weak.

Like it or not, we all tend to generalize at times because we haven't got the time to explore things thoroughly. If you purchase three apples from a store barrel and they're all rotten you tend to feel that the whole barrel is full of rotten apples. You may be right or you may be wrong but why take a chance? This is how generalizations get their power to convince.

## FAULTY ANALOGY

An analogy is a correspondence in some respects between things otherwise dissimilar, such as "a ninety year old and a twelve year old both like to swim". They have love of the sport in common, but not physical capabilities.

The more dissimilar things being compared are the more faulty the analogy. If a Navy poster claimed that it was safer to be in the Navy than to be a resident of New York City, the analogy would be quite faulty. The Navy would be comparing death rates that are not comparable. Only generally young and healthy men and women are admitted into the Navy while New York City has the complete range humans from babies to senior citizens. When a Navy person gets old or severely ill he or she is discharged and returns to the general population. Of course the death rate is greater in New York City than in the Navy, but such an argument, while rather silly, might be persuasive to many young people.

## CONDEMNING THE ORIGIN

This technique attempts to discredit an idea by showing that it has an unappealing source.

One example of this technique would be a claim made by an advocate for the abolition of the death penalty. Such a claim might sound like this; 'The prison system and capital punishment are children of the Dark Ages and should be abolished'.

Another example comes from the history of Nazi Germany. Adolf Hitler was not receptive to any proposals from his scientists for embarking on a nuclear bomb project. He considered nuclear physics to be a "Jewish" science. Any German scientist who showed respect for people like Albert Einstein, a Jew, would be labeled as a "white Jew". In Hitler's condemnation of the source of scientific ideas about nuclear weapons, he ignored what would be the greatest secret weapon of World War II.

I can remember hearing people condemn our use of Dr. Werner von Braun for his ideas and organizing ability in America's guided missile development program on the grounds that the good doctor was Adolf Hitler's rocket scientist.

## FALSE CONVERSION OF PROPOSITIONS

A propagandist will start with a true proposition and end up with one that does not follow. A person who states that all communists are atheists and goes on to say that therefore all atheists are communists is demonstrating the use of this technique.

The statement, "All Roman Catholics believe in God", followed by "All those people who believe in God are Roman Catholics." would probably not be as easily accepted as the first example might be.

## WHAT IS TRUE OF THE PARTS IS TRUE OF THE WHOLE

This is an old logical fallacy that continues to be used today. Let's say that a hater of a governor of one of America's states wants to get him out of office. The hater could search out a few negative features of the governor's administration and go on to draw the conclusion that the governor deserved to be recalled from office.

An automobile salesperson might put down a competitor's car by selecting a few weaknesses in the car and drawing the conclusion that it's a lemon.

Taking a different slant on things a Neo-Nazi could argue that Adolf Hitler loved animals, especially his dog, was loyal to his friends such as Benito Mussolini and won a medal for bravery in World War I (a German Jewish officer recommended Adolf for an iron cross). When the Neo-Nazi claims that these facts show how good and great the Fuehrer was you would most likely hold your nose. The fact is that this is an extreme example of the fallacy. This technique might get a better reception if it were used against or for someone less well known.

## THE BLACK AND WHITE FALLACY

A statement that doesn't allow for intermediate states between two extremes is often a black and white fallacy.

For instance, if people are being described as being good or bad, patriotic or unpatriotic, skinny or fat, tall or short, having thick hair or being bald, a believer or infidel, for or against, just or unjust or happy or sad, the propagandist is using this black and white fallacy.

Of course there are some polarized terms that are valid. For instance a woman is either pregnant or not pregnant. A man or woman is either dead or alive.

## USING AN ILLICIT DEFINITION

This technique involves using a word that has an old and accepted definition and giving the word a new and often unrecognized definition.

Examples:

"If you have an abortion and terminate the life of a potential human being, you are guilty of murder." This use of the word "murder" is flaunting the accepted legal definition.

Alcohol is a drug and anyone selling it is a drug dealer. Liquor store owners should be imprisoned." Here the propagandist is trying to confuse the issue. Alcohol is not an illegal drug in the United States, whereas some other drugs are.

## FALLACY OF BIASED SAMPLING

A propagandist may issue millions of questioners but if his or her sampling is biased, there'll be misleading results. This may lead to false conclusions.

In 1936, before the presidential election, the Reader's Digest magazine distributed millions of questioners in order to attempt to forecast whether Landon or Roosevelt would win the upcoming contest. Peoples' names and addresses were randomly chosen from telephone directories and club membership lists.

In the Great Depression period, many people didn't have telephones and weren't listed in the telephone directories, weren't members of clubs and therefore weren't contacted. This group of urban and rural poor overwhelmingly supported Roosevelt.

Some 2 1/2 million responses to the Reader's Digest questioners were received by the magazine, all indicating a Landon victory. The magazine predicted a win by Landon over Roosevelt. It didn't happen – Roosevelt won. The biased sampling was flawed making the results invalid. The Reader's Digest lost a great degree of its former credibility due to careless sampling.

A propagandist might still go ahead and conduct a biased poll in which the responses would have been designed to support the propagandist's position. The attempt to influence others in this way would be just one of many examples of the principle of using any means to achieve the desired end.

## THE GAMBLER'S FALLACY

People often reason that if they've had a spell of bad luck, they should increase their bets. They feel this way because they assume that they are due for a spell of good luck to balance things out.

A propagandist can make use of the Gambler's Fallacy. If you are running for high office against an opponent who has experienced a run of bad luck, or has made unfortunate mistakes you have an opportunity. You can shout to your audience that you'll change things and bring back happy days. You might say that it's about time that the people's fortunes were changed. You could add to this by saying that we all certainly deserve a win after a series of losses. You will hope that the people will go for this message just like some gamblers do.

## THE FALLACY OF INCONSISTENCY

This fallacy of inconsistency occurs when we reason from inconsistent premises.

<u>Example:</u>

When a propagandist claims that a fetus is a person with an absolute right to life and goes on to say that an abortion is morally wrong except in cases of rape and incest, he or she is reasoning from inconsistent premises.

## APPEAL TO INAPPROPRIATE AUTHORITY

When alleged experts are not in a position to know or are otherwise unreliable, the propagandist is appealing to inappropriate authority.

In the mass media this technique is being used quite often. In a commercial designed to encourage people to drink beer, a movie star or athlete will beat out a brew master every time in touting the greatness of the beverage.

# SECTION 2 – TECHNIQUES OF DIVERSION OR EVASION

## USE OF AMBIGUOUS WORDS

An ambiguous word is one that is susceptible of multiple interpretations. Words such as God, good, freedom, democracy and truth can have many different meanings. By failing to properly define terms, a propagandist can appear to be saying something very concrete when in fact he or she may be saying little of substance. People tend to supply their own definitions of terms and can readily be taken in by a manipulating speaker or writer.

In the statement, "John Smith is a very good candidate," critical thinkers should want some serious discussion of exactly what is meant by the word good.

I once went to a meeting in a church held by a prominent anticommunist organization. The speaker featured at this evening event, open to the public, was an enthusiastic opponent of communism. When question time came around, I asked the speaker if he would kindly define the word communist. He didn't answer that question. I had the feeling that he wanted to be able to label anyone or anything he didn't like as communist.

Quite often a propagandist can get away with using ambiguous words and their use is alive and well to judge from observing the mass media.

**AD HOMINEM**

In Latin ad hominem means "to the man". In today's world it means "to attack a person with words". This technique calls for the abandonment of reason in argument and instead attacking the character of a person. If carried to an extreme, it often results in a poor outcome for the user. Engaging in ad hominem attacks is often referred to as mud slinging.

**BEGGING THE QUESTION**

Begging the question assumes that something not yet proven is true. If the audience lets the propagandist get away with it, begging the question can be an effective technique.

Some Examples:

"Our founding fathers would have never supported the regulation of firearms." (How do we know what the founding fathers would or would not have supported?)

"The future course America must follow is technology, technology, and ever more technology" (The speaker must be pressed to offer some evidence in support of his or her claim.)

"God is on our side." (Prove this and you've done the impossible!)

"History has shown that we must make preemptive strikes against our enemies." (History shows us very little.)

In all of these statements the conclusions are subject to the rigors of proof. Of course the propagandist will conveniently pay no mind to this requirement of critical thinking.

## THE WICKED ALTERNATIVE

Using this technique the propagandist tries to defend someone or something by attacking its opposite.

A propagandist who proclaimed that "We must immediately undertake a massive program of building both a light and a heavy railway system as well as subway systems in all the large cities" will support his position by attacking private transportion. He or she might claim that our present "car culture", with its millions of automobiles, has given us great numbers of deaths and horrible injuries. Continuing the attack, the propagandist might claim that the medical system has been severely stressed. The pollution problem and the waste of much good land for ever growing highway systems might also be advanced.

Sometimes propagandists will set up a decoy, either a person or a thing, that is made to seem so bad and unacceptable that the alternative, backed by the propagandist, looks good. If a real estate salesperson shows you a terrible high priced house that is being used as a decoy, that next house you see may look so much better than the first that you unthinkingly reach for your checkbook.

## NON - SEQUITUR

Non-sequitur is a diversionary technique in which a person seems to be answering a question but, in fact, isn't. Imagine a mother wanting to know what went on during her daughter's first date:

Mother:        "How was your date with Harry?"

Daughter:      "Mom, you should have seen Harry's car! Dad would have loved it. It had a television in the back and four loudspeakers for the stereo. To ride in that car was like riding on a cloud."

In this exchange it's doubtful that the mother was concerned about Harry's car. She was trying to find out about other matters and her daughter knew it.

## ACCUSING THE ACCUSER

This is a way to attempt to fend off an attack by making a diversion. The minute the propagandist is accused of something, he or she fires off a counter accusation.

Example:

Senator A:     " You spend too much of the taxpayers' money"!

Senator B:     "What about that fact finding trip you and your wife took to Europe?"

## NAME CALLING

This is an unsophisticated and demeaning technique to use. It is used by propagandists who feel that their audience is made up of simple minded, rather unthinking people. I recommend not using this technique but in its stead offer reasons and evidence that support your views.

Dr. Josef Goebbels the Nazi propaganda chief used name-calling against

Jews in Germany and throughout the world. He labeled Jews as "untermenschen" or sub-

humans. The Nazis didn't have an exclusive ownership of this technique. Winston Churchill, the

Prime Minister of Great Britain during World War II, called Hitler a "bloodthirsty gutter snipe."

People, places and things have been the recipients of this primitive name-calling technique. (By

the way, my use of the word primitive to describe this technique could be labeled as name-calling.)

Some Examples of Name-Calling:

| | |
|---|---|
| For People: | dirty rat, black dog, vermin, vipers, gutter snipes, uncouth, vulgar, crude, Neanderthal, scum, slime ball, jerk, idiot, imbecile, bitch, witch, fool |
| For Places: | Hell hole, the pits, a dump, the boondocks, a jungle, a snake pit, a shark tank, the sticks, a mud hole, a slum, no place, a zoo, an insane asylum |
| For Things: | Outrageous, primitive, crude, ugly, useless, horrible, nasty, inferior, stupid, bizarre, ridiculous, a "rube goldberg" |

**THE USE OF SATIRE**

Satire is attacking human vices and follies through wit. Satire is used to attack those

conventional ideas and practices that are thought to be absurdities in the opinion of the satirist. The

vices usually chosen as targets by satirists are those considered to be blindly accepted by people through thoughtlessness, habit or social custom. The distance between how things are and how they should be is revealed by the satirist.

A few subjects for satire are prejudice, lack of foresight, quest for total security, war, crime, cruelty, impatience, disloyalty, pride, sloth, lust, envy, greed, anger, gluttony and the list goes on.

An example of satirical writing which attacks the folly of an individual's search for extreme personal security is shown in the following essay.

Security Forever

Justin Smythe lived in a very large American city and he was scared out of his wits. The crime rate in his town was high and steadily increasing. He saw himself and his family in extreme danger.

Justin went on to make a decision to do something to protect himself and his family from evil doers. He installed a television camera to constantly sweep the area in front of his house. He was especially proud of the expert way he placed two automatic 50 caliber machine guns to cover his front door. Land mines were cleverly placed under the front lawn. "Flame throwers" would get anyone foolishly attempting to climb an exterior wall. The backyard was the perfect place for his six pit traps with sharp spears embedded in their bases – a little something along with jungle fever that he picked on his stint in Vietnam. Barbed wire supplemented the electrified fence that was protecting the rear of the property. Bulletproof glass was used to replace the ordinary windowpanes.

All of these security systems weren't cheap. There was no more going out to restaurants, movies, concerts or taking vacations. Even ordering a pizza was out of the question, but for a different reason!

There were some savings at first. The family dog Bonzo fell into one of the backyard pits while he was chasing a cat. That ended the purchasing of pet food and paying for a yearly license. Things got a little rough when Justin's mother-in-law made an unannounced visit and was cut down by the two machine guns at the front door. When the mailperson stepped on a front lawn land mine, Justin was arrested, tried and thrown into prison for a long stretch.

The lawsuits that followed led to some more unfortunate incidents in Justin's life. He was forced sell his house and surrender his life savings. His wife divorced him and the kids don't come to visit daddy. However, there's one bright spot in all of these happenings. He doesn't worry too much about intruders where he lives now.

## REPARTEE

Repartee is an exchange of quick witty replies to sharp or bitter remarks. Only outstandingly clever propagandists should try this technique.

Examples:

Gladstone vs. Disraeli (members of the British government)

Gladstone:     "You'll either die from a hangman's noose or from a social disease."

Disraeli:       "That depends on whether I embrace your principles or your mistress."

Lady Nancy Astor, who entered the House of Commons in 1919 as its first woman member, had few betters in the art of vicious repartee. But she did have some and Winston Churchill was one of them. After one conflict over ideas, Lady Astor is reported to have said to Churchill, "Winston, if you were my husband, I would poison your coffee." Churchill replied, "If you were my wife, Nancy, I would drink it."

Reportedly, Isadora Duncan approached George Bernard Shaw with the proposal that they should have a child. She thought that the combination of her looks and his brains would be impressive. Shaw supposedly countered by saying that it might go the other way – her brains and his looks.

## CHOOSE A SCAPEGOAT

Scapegoat is a term used to focus the blame, correctly or incorrectly, on one group. History is strewn with groups used as scapegoats, especially ethnic, religious, racial or social class. These groups were blamed for all or most of the ills of a particular society.

In Nazi Germany, Jews became the scapegoats for that nation's numerous problems. In Turkey during the period of World War I, Armenian Christians were blamed for that nation's troubles. In Indonesia, especially after World War II, Chinese were blamed for troubles. Many African tribal groups in South Africa blamed Hindus for economic problems. In the United States the Ku Klux Klan blamed Jews, Catholics and others for all of Americas problems. The list of scapegoats seems endless.

A propagandist can set up a scapegoat to take the blame for almost any problem. Here is a list of some common problems accompanied by their related scapegoats:

High prices:  corporate greed, labor unions demand for higher wages

Poor medical care:  drug companies, greedy doctors

Suburban sprawl:  white flight, land developers, highway interests

Environmental problems:  overpopulation, the automobile, big business

Almost any problem you can think of has more than one cause.  Blaming one thing for a problem is a way of diverting attention from what may be the actual cause or causes of the problem

## SECTION 3- TECHNIQUES THAT APPEAL TO THE EMOTIONS

**APPEAL TO TRADITION**

This technique appeals to people who use historical precedent to judge ideas. All of us , at some point, have heard people say, "But we've always done it that way." This attitude works against innovation and change.

Here are two examples of the use of this technique:

Those who are against gun control could argue that our founding fathers would have fought any attempts to restrict the use of firearms.

Military historians often remark that nations are usually prepared for the next war based on what went on in the last war. Many times these nations are caught off guard by innovations. Adolf Hitler felt that the air force should be built around fighter planes as in World War I. He felt that jet planes were a waste of time. The world might have been in for sad times if the Fuhrer hadn't been so tradition bound.

Have we outgrown appeals to tradition? Certainly not and a propagandist can often get loud applause by appealing to the values that sustained our nation through good and bad times in the past.

## DEMAND FOR SPECIAL CONSIDERATION

This technique is usually based on a hardship story. Politicians and lawyers are well known for making pleas for special circumstances to get someone or something off the hook.

The following is a list of selected areas from which hardship stories may emerge:

Gender, race, political groups, religion, mental or physical disabilities, height, weight, social class, regional background, sexual orientation, occupation, past record of behavior, temporary mental state, membership in an organization etc.

A politician might argue that strong gun controls would constitute a hardship on farmers and ranchers who cannot protect their crops and herds from predators without the unrestricted purchase and use of firearms.

You can imagine a lawyer arguing for a lighter sentence for his client based on that client's past good behavior. The lawyer might claim that a severe sentence would be truly hard on a person who has only slipped once from the straight and narrow path.

## APPEAL TO THE EMOTIONS

Human emotions constitute a very complex set of feelings. The range of emotions is extensive and each emotion can be subdivided into seemingly endless variations.

Emotions can be compared to colors. A person can choose one color and by adding increasing amounts of white he or she can create endless tints of color. If a person adds increasing amounts of black to the chosen color he or she can create endless shades of the color.

Love can be subdivided into compassion, fondness, obsessive attachment, adoration and so forth. Fear can be subdivided into terror, apprehension, uneasiness and countless phobias attached to an infinite list of objects and situations.

One way of thinking about emotions is to list some of them under two headings: Positive Emotions and Negative Emotions.

Positive Emotions: love, hope, faith, enthusiasm, loyalty, pity, remorse, etc.

Negative Emotions: unreasonable fear, jealousy, anger, revenge, greed, envy, arrogance, etc.

Let's look at four examples that involve an appeal to the emotions.

### An Appeal for Pity

Humans are capable of feeling pity or sympathy for the misfortunes of others. A lawyer can tap into this feeling and often get a jury to either reduce his or her client's sentence or possibly acquit him or her.

Demonstrating that a murderer had an abusive childhood is not an unusual ploy used by lawyers in the nation's courtrooms. This appeal will seldom work if the plea for mercy doesn't have some basis in fact that makes the appeal seem reasonable. An accused murderer of his parents might make a plea for mercy on the grounds that he or she is now orphaned but it would most likely meet with rejection by the average jury.

There are two famous appeals for pity made by American political leaders.

In 1944, some Republicans accused President Roosevelt of sending a heavy destroyer to the Aleutian Islands to pick up his pet dog Fala, a Scottish terrier. The president was outraged and made a speech in which he said something to the effect that he and his family didn't resent attacks but his little dog Fala did. Republican critics were silenced by the sympathetic response of the American people.

In 1952, Richard Nixon was accused by Democrats of dipping into a party "slush fund" for personal expenses. Some of his fellow Republicans thought a scandal was in the making. To save his vice-presidential candidacy, Nixon made a speech on September 23, 1952 defending himself by saying he hadn't been feathering his own nest. He acknowledged receiving several gifts which could be returned, but he vowed to keep Checkers, a cocker spaniel that was a gift to his daughters. The American public felt sympathetic to him and he went on to become the vice-president. This became known as the "Checkers Speech".

An Appeal Based on Remorse:

A lawyer can try to show his or her client has remorse for the crime he or she has committed. Sometimes this will sway the jury resulting in a lighter sentence for the accused. You'll see this technique in any visit to a criminal court.

An Appeal to Greed:

Greed seems to be a universal characteristic of people everywhere. A mayor of a small town with economic problems might request the community's support for constructing a prison. The mayor might claim that new jobs would be created, taxes would be lowered and town businesses would profit by the expected increase in economic activity brought about by the new prison. The opposition to the project would have a hard time fighting the mayor, I suspect.

An Appeal to Fear:

Fear is one of the most basic emotional states. It is an excellent choice for any propagandist's appeal to emotions. A Xenophobic politician might argue that we should seal off our borders to immigrants before Americans become overrun by foreigners who don't share our values, don't act within the law and take jobs from our children.

To witness a play on several emotions simultaneously, one only has to observe the behavior of apocalyptic cults. These "end of the world" groups are usually always after recruits and their group leaders generally play on fear but at the same time offer hope, meaning and purpose. Vulnerable people seeking a firm foundation of belief in something greater than themselves are often taken in by these cults.

Once recruited the cult leaders often work on feelings of shame and/or guilt in order to manipulate (brainwash) members. This approach can work with all groups, not just apocalyptic cults. A salesperson offering a set of encyclopedias, or encyclopedic software, can use shame/guilt to encourage parents to buy things for the benefit of their children. Adolf Hitler used the shame of Germany's defeat in World War I to move his audiences. The American president, J.F. Kennedy, said in his inaugural address of January 20, 1961, "…ask not what your country can do for you – ask what you can do for your country." He was using shame/guilt to try to motivate his fellow Americans.

An effective propagandist, appealing to the emotions, deliberately shows his or her emotional feelings to an audience. If the propagandist is delivering an uplifting speech, a show of joy and enthusiasm is in order. If a somber message filled with warnings and dire predictions of a hazardous future is being given, then the emotions of the propagandist must credibly support the necessary mood of sadness, doom and gloom.

People generally like to see a speaker who displays an emotional commitment to the ideas, issues and principles being transmitted to listeners and/or readers.

## PERSONIFICATION

Personification is giving human characteristics to something that is non-human.

In World War II, American propaganda posters portrayed Japanese soldiers as large rats eagerly feeding on the victims of their conquests. They were giving the rats the characteristics of an enemy.

In advertising there are numerous animals given the power of speech. When some young children see a pet Chihuahua they expect it to speak. Dogs speak in the television commercials don't they?

An environmentalist might say that acid rain is whispering in our ears, "Take care of the environment or the environment will take care of you. "

## THE USE OF HOT AND COLD WORDS

Emotion packed words or, as I call them, hot words, carry great power to arouse strong feelings in people. On the other hand, the choice of relatively unemotional or, as I call them, cold words, can reduce strong feelings. When you hear that an ex-convict has just purchased a home next door to you, the word itself can have a strong negative effect on you. The substitution of a word such as non-conformist for ex-convict might lesson your apprehension level.

The clever propagandist chooses his or her words carefully hoping to persuade people to think a certain way. Two examples of how hot and cold words could be selected follows:

Example a:

Several young boys are dead and you, as the defense attorney for the alleged perpetrators of the crime, want to cool down the jury and reduce any strong feelings they might already have. On the other side is the prosecuting attorney who really wants a conviction of the alleged felons and wants to increase the emotional intensity of the jurors. A hot and cold mixed word list follows:

killed

murdered

butchered

massacred

executed

liquidated

terminated

martyred

have slain

slaughtered

They         the boys.

You can make your own choice as to which words are hot or cold.

Example b:

In this case a witness for the prosecution has been caught telling a lie to the jury. The prosecuting attorney wants to defend the witness while the defense attorney wants to do just the opposite. They each must choose words appropriate to their goals.

told an outright lie

told a falsehood

told a story

told a fib

|          | told an untruth                |             |
|----------|--------------------------------|-------------|
| He or she | made an unwarranted assertion | to the jury |
|          | told a nursery tale            |             |
|          | trumped up a story             |             |
|          | told a white lie               |             |
|          | made an unfounded declaration  |             |
|          | related a false statement      |             |

Once again, you choose which words or hot or cold.

Instead of offensive words a speaker or writer can choose to use euphemisms, words that are less offensive.

Examples:

| Offensive Terms   | Euphemisms               |
|-------------------|--------------------------|
| Homeless          | residentially challenged |
| Mortuary room     | slumber room             |
| Poor student      | educationally challenged |
| Slums             | poor environments        |
| Blast the enemy   | pacify the enemy         |
| Toilet            | restroom                 |
| Sex show          | adult entertainment      |
| 12,000,000 killings | final solution         |

| | |
|---|---|
| toilet paper | bathroom tissue |
| kill the dog | put the dog to sleep |
| fired | selected out |
| naughty lawbreaker | severe norm violator |
| false teeth | dentures |
| breast meat | white meat |

You get the idea!  The following two passages will show how euphemisms can put a different slant on a story.

## Euphemistic Passage

Wally was a severe norm violator who lived in a poor environment.  As a residentially challenged youth he spent much time at adult entertainment centers.  When he was arrested for liberating women's purses, he used many expletives and made a pre-emptive strike against a police person.  Even though he was educationally challenged, he vowed that given a chance he would become a tonsorial artist.

## Translation

Wally was a naughty little lawbreaker who lived in a slum.  As a homeless youth he spent much time at sex show places.  When he was arrested for stealing women's purses, he swore and made a sneak attack on a policeperson. Even though he was a poor student, he vowed that given a chance he would become a barber.

**LOOK TO THE FUTURE AND BE OPTIMISTIC**

Propagandists can take advantage of people's desire to picture the future as being bright and prosperous. Words and phrases such as innovation, progress, advancement, improvement, high technology, ever upward and onward, reaching the stars, problem solving, high hopes, the bright world of tomorrow, etc. can form a positive attitude in the minds of many.

This technique can work best if the propagandist isn't overly optimistic. A few obstacles should be included in the portrayal of a rosy future.

## LET ALTRUISM REIGN

Altruism is concern for the welfare of others as opposed to egoism and selfishness. Many Americans have always thought they were a generous and magnanimous people. They try to help others whenever disasters such as earthquakes, fierce storms, great fires and floods occur.

Telling the audience how generous and caring they are builds up their self-esteem and helps get the message across.

# SECTION 4 -TECHNIQUES THAT INVOLVE FALSEHOOD OR TRICKERY

## QUOTING OUT OF CONTEXT

This technique distorts the meaning of what a person has said about someone or something. The propagandist selects a few words to omit from a given text so as to distort the original meaning. Let's say that the book <u>Hot Cargo</u> has been reviewed in a newspaper. The review read "<u>Hot Cargo</u> is the best example of an amateurish film released this year." A later advertisement for the film, appropriately altered by the propagandist reads, "<u>Hot Cargo</u> is the best...film released this year." When most people see three dots in a sentence, they seldom check out the original sentence to locate omitted words. It helps to be cautious about accepting messages with three dots as completely factual.

## USE OF NUMBERS TO IMPRESS

Numbers seem to impress many people. In my state of California as the lotto prize figures climb, the sale of tickets increases. Lower dividend figures often impress stockholders in a negative way. Population growth used to be the pride of cities, states and nations as if numbers alone affirmed the greatness of a place.

Some corporations brag about the number of items sold to validate what they manufacture. Prosecuting attorneys of alleged criminals like to mention the number of previous convictions of the accused. The use of numbers can present a false impression of having the facts and being scientific about the points you are trying to make.

**FALSE DILEMMA**

A dilemma is a situation that requires one to choose between two equally balanced alternatives. What makes a dilemma false is when only two choices are presented to a person or group, though in fact there are several or many possible choices. A person trying to persuade others knows full well the range of choices but wants to distract the listener by offering seemingly restricted choices.

This technique is illustrated by a political slogan from Denmark in 1935. The slogan "Stauning Eller Kaos" (Stauning Or Chaos) was taken from an election poster of the period and presented the voter with only two choices.

This false dilemma was not confined to Denmark, but seemed to be a common strategy for dictators throughout the world of the 1930s. You'll see it used today.

**USING A MINOR POINT TO DISCREDIT A PERSON, PLACE OR THING**

This technique tries to make a mountain out of a molehill. In debating, speakers may try desperately to disprove a minor point or seize upon a small matter to discredit their opponent. An automobile salesperson may bring up one small weakness in a competitor's car, such as a lack of leather covered seats, to discredit the whole vehicle.

Using this technique requires caution. If the small point the propagandist brings to light seems like nit-picking, the audience might discredit him or her!

*Henry T. Conserva*

## LEADING QUESTION

A leading question is one that, no matter how it is answered, will incriminate the one who answers. A lawyer I once knew said that, in court, you can win a case through "clever" questioning. Never ask a question that doesn't get the answer you want. Examples of leading questions are as follows:

a.      Have you stopped beating your wife?

b.      Did you stop your habit of substance abuse?

c.      Have you stopped committing acts of treason?

## SEEK SIMPLE ANSWERS

Demanding a simple answer is a device used by advertisers, politicians and lawyers. For example, a person might hear this question in a television commercial of an automobile company, "Do you want to see the world's best sedan today?" The advertiser wants a quick affirmative reaction from the viewer. The advertiser does not want a person to research the qualities of the car in a consumer magazine to seek out an evaluation before coming to the showroom.

A politician, after discussing a few examples of outrageous crimes in his or her district might ask the audience, "Do you want to put a stop to crime?" Easier said then done, but he or she hopes to develop an image of being tough on crime issues.

A lawyer for a union of factory workers might well ask a jury, "Do we want to stop all immigration to the United States? I say Yes!, what do you say?" This is a simplistic appeal to a

32

thorny and complex question which needs extensive discussion and examination. The lawyer wants a quick response from the jury and hopefully a positive one for his point of view.

## EXAGGERATION OF CONSEQUENCES

Exaggerating the consequences that may follow from the acceptance of someone or something isn't liked, or the rejection of someone or something that is liked is a common debate tactic.

One candidate for public office might claim that if his or her opponent is elected taxes would increase, the budget would be in a shambles and corruption would invade every agency of the government.

An advocate of slow or no growth in a community might react to a proposal from a developer to build new housing by making exaggerations. He or she might say that if new housing is built schools will be so crowded that students will forfeit their education, roads will become parking lots and the environmental damage done by the project will be irreparable.

## DOUBLE TALK

Double talk is meaningless speech. It can consist of nonsense words or misplaced words within intelligible speech, or it can simply be contradictory statements.

Some propagandists say two things at once in a contradiction. A hypothetical dictator might say that he or she will end a war but he or she will not just stand around and see his or her friends' overrun. The implication here is the dictator will actually remain at war.

A governor of a state might give a speech in which he or she encourages more state support for the state's system of higher education. In the same speech the governor might call for cutting college budgets in order to give tax cuts to the state's taxpayers. All this represents an attempt to try to please two sections of the electorate. Sometimes this kind of double talk fails to please either party.

## MANIPULATING NUMBERS

This technique uses numbers to deceive. There are many forms of manipulation and I've selected a few to examine.

Countries with low productivity can deceive by showing the percentage of growth in the production of a selected item rather than present the actual number of an item that was produced.

### Telephones Produced

|          | 1998    | 1999    | % of Increase |
|----------|---------|---------|---------------|
| Nation A | 1       | 2       | 100%          |
| Nation B | 100,000 | 125,000 | 25%           |

This ploy skips the numbers and leads a person into looking at the percentage figures only.

When a person hears a commercial that states that 4 out of 5 doctors do something or use something such as take out insurance or drink a popular beverage, the intent is often to deceive. The advertisers only have to find 4 doctors who use a product or service and 1 who doesn't. Listeners or viewers are supposed to think that thousands of doctors were asked to respond to a survey.

In mathematics there are three types of average, the mean, the mode and the median. The mean is the sum of a group of quantities divided by the number of quantities. For example, the mean average of 6, 8, 12, 14, and 20 is 12 or 60 divided by 5. The mode average is the number that occurs most frequently in a group. The median average is a number that divides a group in half according to size.

Let's pretend to be a real estate salesperson examining a group of homes for sale in a hypothetical community. I'll give the number of homes followed by the asking price. One home for $1,000,000, six homes for $350,000 each, twenty homes for $300,000 each, nine homes for $250,000 each, three homes for $200,000 each, two homes for $150,000 each, six homes for $125,000 each, five homes for $95,000 each and eleven homes for 85,000 each represents the current available housing stock.

In this group of homes the mean average selling price is $469,000, the mode average is $300,000 and the median average is $250,000.

If the realtor had a wealthy client with repulsive personality traits that might cause difficulties within the community, the realtor could present that client with the median average price of homes. The realtor might suggest the client look at a more upscale neighborhood. On the other hand, if the realtor has a relatively poor buyer who wouldn't fit well into the community, the realtor could mention the mean average price which might discourage the client's search for a home in that locale. This is a sophisticated way of persuading people through the manipulation of numbers.

## BIG LIE

Big lies are sometimes referred to as being factoids. Factoids are assertions of fact with no evidence to support them. Adolf Hitler used the big lie technique. The idea is that if a lie is big enough, people will tend to think there must be some truth in it. Hitler falsely told the German people that Polish forces had assaulted German army units in an unprovoked attack. Many Germans asked, "Why doesn't Adolf Hitler do something about this?" He did and World War II began.

The big lie was used a lot before Hitler's rise to power. In World War I the British spread the word that the Germans were cutting off the hands of Belgian children. This was not true.

## PLACEMENT OF EMPHASIS

A positive or negative spin can be put on most things. It all depends on what is to be emphasized.

A person might take pride in the fact that say 85% of American homes have indoor plumbing. A detractor of America could stress the fact that 15% of American homes do not have indoor plumbing.

Perhaps a teacher gives his or her class a 100 question examination. A well-liked student might be praised for getting 84 correct answers. A disliked student might be told that he or she answered 16 questions incorrectly.

This technique works fairly well because the facts aren't altered on any topic but puts a spin on things.

## USE INNUENDO

An innuendo is implying an accusation without risking refutation by actually saying it. If a person were to hear this statement, "The captain was sober today!" it implies that he's usually drunk. If the propagandist wants to throw a sugar-covered dart at someone or something, then innuendo is effective.

Another slant on this technique is for the propagandist to say he or she isn't saying something and then goes ahead and says it. Some sample statements are, "I'm not saying you're fat but you could lose some weight." And "I'm not calling you a liar, but you should tell the truth."

## APPEAL TO IGNORANCE

The principle of this technique is that if something can't be proven it is not so, then it is so. It used to be difficult to prove that cigarettes were bad for a person's health. Court cases against tobacco companies used to be consistently lost. The tobacco companies were always saying that smoking didn't constitute a health problem, and nobody could prove them wrong.

During World War II, Japanese-Americans were rounded up and placed in internment camps. If they couldn't prove that they were not spying for Japan, many government officials considered that, in fact, they were spying. In the atmosphere of hate in 1942 too few Americans were willing to take a chance on the loyalty of Japanese-Americans.

A recent example of this technique would be illustrated by the controversy about the influence of violent scenes in motion pictures and on television. The idea is that if you can't prove that violence on television and in the motion pictures makes viewers violent, then these media programs don't make people violent.

## CARD STACKING

Only listing the good, or bad, features of a person, place or thing is card stacking. This is really a way of telling a lie by telling the truth, but not the whole truth.

For example an automobile salesperson can distort the truth in order to make a sale.

### Characteristics of a Hypothetical Automobile

Good body construction, engine subject to breakdown, inferior radiator, good carburetor, poor electrical wiring, large and convenient back luggage trunk, poor instrumentation, excellent brakes, poor ignition, comfortable seats, low quality interior lighting, poor mileage, excellent sun roof.

A person can be sure that a potential customer will be presented with all the underlined characteristics of the car.

Commercials often contain this card stacking technique, but you'll find it used by almost every propagandist.

**STRESS HIGH MORAL PRINCIPLES**

This technique claims that high moral principles (a vague term) characterize the people, ideas or things the propagandist supports. E.g., "My support of Dick Smith for governor is based on his strict adherence to the high moral principles so beautifully expressed by our founding fathers." Many people like to think they are moral and uphold the values dominant in their communities

**FALSE URGENCY**

Doctors often tell their patients not to rush about so much, but advertisers seem deaf to such advice. A person constantly hears commercials calling for customers to rush down to the store before all items are sold out. If the customers blindly obeyed all of these appeals they'd die from cardiac arrest. People are made to fear that they'll be left out in the cold on bargain sales (greed rears its head again).

**PRAISE ONE THING THE OPPONENT HAS DONE. THEN ON TO THE ATTACK**

The propagandist can praise one small thing either said or done by his or her opponent and thereby appear to be fair-minded and rather magnanimous. The propagandist also gives the appearance of avoiding the descent into mud slinging. After his or her initial goodwill gesture or concession, the opposition will be picked apart.

# MAKING A MINOR CONFESSION AND SAYING THAT NOW YOU'VE SEEN THE LIGHT

In a speech a propagandist could announce that he or she thought like the opponent, but now sees things differently. This should make the opposition appear to be somewhat backward and reluctant to change his or her position in the light of new evidence. If things go well, the propagandist could come off as a reasonable person who is willing to change after a careful examination of a problem or issue.

# SET UP A STRAW MAN

A straw man is a fabricated person, object or matter (issue) used as a purposely weak adversary in a debate.

If a political propagandist is opposed to illegal immigration into the United States, he or she can fabricate a stereotypical illegal immigrant with outlandish and exaggerated characteristics. The fabricated individual will possess an astonishing number of bad tendencies such as criminal behavior (an illegal entry into the United States for example), an inability to read, write or speak English, a willingness to take jobs away from legal immigrants, an eager consumer of welfare funds, etc. This hypothetical straw man would be easy to attack in a debate on the rights of illegal immigrants.

A debate on the importance of greater funding for NASA would lend itself to the use of the straw man technique by propagandists opposed to the space agency. The International Space Station project would become the straw man in the debate. It can be called a waste of our national resources, an unending costly experiment, a drain on other science projects and a publicity stunt for NASA.

The fact that there is some opposition to the project makes it relatively difficult to defend as opposed to other NASA projects.

The matter of bilingual education can be argued using the straw man approach. Those opposed to bilingual education can claim that it hinders the learning of English by non-English speaking newcomers to America. The young immigrants will not get good jobs because of their poor English skills. Also, they won't be able to fully participate in the political process of their newly adopted nation. It could be pointed out that bilingual education will produce a flood of future welfare recipients. Obviously the propagandist has made the matter of bilingual education into a monstrous calamity.

The essence of the straw man technique is to exaggerate and/or distort the opponent's argument in order to make it seem illogical or unreasonable.

## TELLING THEM YOU WERE GOING TO LIE, BUT COULDN'T DO IT

The propagandist must exercise caution trying this one. It helps if he or she has some acting ability. If done well, the audience might be better disposed to accept the message. People like speakers who at least give the appearance of leveling with them.

For example, a hypothetical mayoral candidate might tell an assembled crowd something like this: "I was going to tell you how great our city is and that it is a role model for other cities in our state. But I can't bring myself to lie to you. You're an intelligent citizenry and both you and I know that this city is in deep trouble. Working together we can turn things around."

## BUILD A "POTEMKIN VILLAGE"

Alexandrovich Gregory Potemkin (1739 – 1791) was a Russian administrator serving Empress Catherine the Great. One of his pet projects was the colonization of the Ukraine. He vastly underestimated the cost of the venture and the project was quite unfinished when Catherine took a tour of the Ukraine.

Potemkin tried to cover up the lack of progress and hide it from the eyes of Empress Catherine. There developed an apocryphal tale of Potemkin erecting artificial villages, like Hollywood stage sets, to be seen by the Empress in passing.

"Potemkin Villages" came to denote any pretentious façade designed to cover up a shabby or undesirable condition. If the propagandist needs to cover up something, this technique may work. "Potemkin Villages" have been built at many times and in many places.

In the pre-Civil War American South, southern life was generally portrayed as being quite wonderful. Plantations were shown to be all but a paradise for slaves. Illustrations showed white washed and curtained slave quarters with men playing banjoes and children happily playing under magnolia trees. This fiction was far from the truth as seen in recollections of ex-slaves that have been recorded

Another example of building a "Potemkin Village" comes from the 1940s. The Nazis built a concentration camp at Theresienstadt in what is now the Czech Republic. It opened in 1941 and closed in 1945 with the allied victory in World War II. The camp, 40 miles from Prague, was built like a little town.  It had a library, a zoo, a symphony orchestra, art classes and workshops and a good cafeteria.

Theresienstadt was periodically scrubbed up to impress visiting Red Cross workers.  Nazi films portrayed the camp as a paradise for the inmates who were something of an elite group of prisoners in Nazi thinking.  Decorated German Jewish soldiers of World War I, Danish Jews and wealthy Jews who paid to avoid being sent to Auschwitz, the most feared death camp, were counted as being lucky.  Eventually luck ran out for many prisoners at Theresienstadt as Germany began to lose the war.  Disease and malnutrition took their toll.

Hypothetically, a propagandist for a president seeking reelection might draft a speech showing an America that is great, strong, rich and beautiful.  The fact that the portrayal is unreal, a "Potemkin Village" probably wouldn't bother him or her at all.

## MAKE THE IDEAS BEING SUPPORTED OR OPPOSED SEEM TO BE FOREGONE CONCLUSIONS

If a propagandist supports a particular presidential candidate, then he or she can speak as though that person is all but in the White House already.  A display of confidence (perhaps overconfidence) often can sway public opinion in support of the propagandist's choice.  Caution: It's true to say that many people supporting other candidates may lose heart feeling that there is no hope for their choices and not go to the polls to cast their votes.  It's equally true to say that many others who support the propagandist's choice may not vote because they become overconfident about the outcome of the election and feel that their votes are not necessary.

*Henry T. Conserva*

In a debate, if a person talks as though his or her opponent's position is wrong beyond question, these words may work to win support for his or her side of a question. We can spot similar demonstrations of confidence in court struggles where contending lawyers clash.

## DEFINE TERMS TO SUIT GOALS

Defining terms the way the propagandist wishes can eliminate things he or she opposes or supports.

Examples:

If a propagandist rates computers higher than books, he or she can push books to the back burner by defining a library as a repository of electronic information. A budget proposal from the propagandist will certainly favor computers over books.

An advocate for a candidate for high public office can define the word "good" to favor his or her choice. As part of a definition of "good" in what makes a "good candidate ", the advocate might include military service. This definition might well exclude from consideration any other candidates who lack a record of military service to the nation.

# SECTION 5 -TECHNIQUES THAT PLAY ON HUMAN BEHAVIORAL TENDENCIES

## APPEAL TO AUTHORITY

Many people don't like being self-directed. Making decisions and thinking for themselves make some people fearful and/or nervous. When someone tells them what to think or do it is quite relaxing. They just do what they're told and abdicate any responsibility for their actions.

In an appeal to authority the propagandist simply tells people what to do or think. Examples would be statements that proclaim, "Drink Milk" or "Join the Army" or "Support Your Party." With this technique the propagandist doesn't have to provide reasons or explanations. People are just supposed to do what they are told.

## REPETITION

Even the thickest skull can be penetrated by a message if it is repeated often enough. It would be wise for the propagandist to repeat the message with some variation. The German dictator, Adolf Hitler, wrote, "The intelligence of the masses is small. Their forgetfulness is great. They must be told the same thing a thousand times." It would appear that many advertisers today agree with him.

During my high school days, a friend of mine rejected the idea that he should study and get good grades. In a class on American government, he refused to take any notes on the teacher's lectures. Instead he read newspapers and magazines quietly at the back of the class. He made no troubles so the teacher never took action against his lack of cooperation.

The teacher's lectures on the Constitution stressed constant repetition. Statements such as "Each state has two senators.", "Supreme Court justices serve life terms.", etc., were repeated frequently. On a Constitution test of multiple choice questions my friend got an A grade. The repeated information had been imbedded in his brain. He failed the course but he learned the effectiveness of repetition as a teaching technique. You'll see repetition in most political and advertising campaigns.

**USE SLOGANS**

The word slogan most likely originated as a battle cry of ancient Scottish or Irish warriors. It is defined as a phrase expressing the aims or nature of an enterprise or organization. The word motto is a synonym for slogan. A slogan can be thought of as an abbreviated idea which, hopefully, will persuade people to think as you want them to think.

One of the most persistent human efforts is for elite groups in any society to try to persuade, brainwash, those members of society lower on the social class structure to think or act in a desired way. What better way to do this than to create a simplified easily remembered statement.

Slogans are not designed to be carefully examined but to be accepted without question. Slogans can be very short or long lived. They can be as short as one word or as long as a brief paragraph. Some are catchy while others are plain and straight forward.

One example of a catchy American slogan comes to us from the mid-nineteenth century. In several cities in America, political parades were held in which the participants were shouting, "Fifty-four forty or fight!" This slogan reflected a goal of President James K. Polk to gain land in the

Oregon Country from Great Britain. The Oregon Controversy between the United States and Great Britain was settled by a compromise in 1846 which resulted in the border between British Columbia, Canada and the United States being drawn at the 49th parallel of latitude.

One of the best slogans that I recently noticed in San Francisco, California was crafted to make street crossings safer for pedestrians. The slogan read, "Feeling run down? You will if you cross at the wrong time buster."

## BANDWAGON

Most people feel comfortable when what they do is also done by many other people. Like kids jumping on a circus bandwagon, people can be swept away by the enthusiasm of a crowd.

I remember a visit I paid to New Orleans. When it came time to have dinner I walked down a street in the famous French Quarter of the city. I looked into one restaurant and saw that there were uniformed waiters with white linen towels draped over their arms. I could see comfortable chairs, beautifully decorated tables, a fine bar and colorful potted plants. There was only one thing missing – customers! As I glanced further on down the street, I saw a long line of customers outside another restaurant. Where do you think I ate dinner that night? You guessed it! I took my place in the line and felt quite comfortable doing it.

Reportedly, a British journalist fluent in German attended a Nazi rally and found himself giving Adolf Hitler a salute with his outstretched right arm as everyone else was doing. The journalist was shocked by his own behavior for he was certainly no supporter of the Fuehrer.

Supporters of a Democrat presidential candidate might say, "Everyone is going Democrat this year." The same claim might be made by a supporter of the Republicans.

## PLAIN FOLKS

This is an appealing technique for politicians, entertainers and spokespersons. If they are regular guys and gals, an average audience appears to like them better. Most people are uncomfortable in the company of very wealthy people, famous personalities or outstanding experts in various fields. Knowing this can work to the benefit of propagandists.

America's presidents, from George Washington, the kid who reportedly chopped down a cherry tree to Abraham Lincoln the rail splitting lawyer and more recently the touch football playing of John F. Kennedy, have demonstrated that they're just regular fellows who act in ways similar to your next door neighbors.

Motion picture magazines and celebrity journals often show the rich and famous of the entertainment world pursuing hobbies, decorating their homes and playing with their children. These activities create a good image in the collective body of fans throughout the world.

Very bright people and outstanding students make many of their fellows nervous. In a history class that I taught in high school, I had an exceptionally outstanding student. He knew all of the answers to the questions given to the class but he seldom raised his hand. In a conversation I had with him, I mentioned his restraint. He volunteered that he didn't want to appear to dominate the class. Later, I found out that he had been elected to be the president of his class. If he had acted as a "know-it-all" I doubt that he would have been so successful in school politics.

**TRANSFER**

This technique attempts to transfer either good or bad feelings the propagandist might have towards a person, place or thing to another person, place or thing.

If people see you in the company of crooks they tend to think of you as a crook. If, on the other hand, you are seen with high status people, you are usually thought to be of high status as well. It's a form of the old saying, "You are judged by the company you keep."

Advertisers use transfer considerably. A group of young and beautiful men and women at a beach are shown drinking a national brand soft drink, viewers or listeners are supposed to transfer their good feelings they have toward the young people to the soft drink.

Anti-smoking advocates will show cigarette smoking people coughing terribly in images that viewers, it is hoped, will transfer to the act of lighting up cigarettes.

**TESTIMONIAL**

This technique makes use of popular well known people to support a person, a product or an idea. An expert is seldom used in making a testimonial advertisement. If the propagandist is trying to sell shoes he or she is much better off using a well known basketball star to support the product than a career shoemaker that few people know. Hero worship trumps reason in many ways.

In politics one important job of a political leader is to make speeches in support of his or her fellow party members who are campaigning for office. Later on the leader can collect I.O.Us from those whom he or she gave testimonials to in the hopes of winning re-election.

## USING A BIAS

A bias is a preference or inclination that inhibits impartial judgement. A bias can slant in two different directions.

Biases may support, condone or praise certain people, places, ideas or things that are considered to be important and positive among a large group of people in a given society.

On the other hand, biases may feature condemnation or opposition to certain people, places, ideas and things that are considered to be evil, destructive or anti-social by a large group of people in a given society.

If a propagandist wants to make use of a bias in a speech or commercial, he or she will have some work to do. The audience should be investigated to uncover any possible biases that can be used to support or attack the issue being debated. Caution is called for after the biases have been discovered so as not to alienate any important segment of the audience.

Every society has its sacred cows, a person, place, idea or thing that is considered to be so important that few people speak out against them. . In Indian society the cow is traditionally held in such high esteem that is has become sacred. Its importance to the community is beyond question. The Hindus generally feel that all animals have souls, but the cow is the most sacred of all animals.

Poor treatment of a cow is considered to be disgraceful behavior and the consumption of beef is avoided by devout Hindus.

One way to identify positive biases, or things many people strongly support, is to look at a few sacred cows in American society.

## Some American Sacred Cows:

### Economic Sacred Cows:

Private property, capitalism, free enterprise, the right to form business

### Political Sacred Cows:

The presidency, the Supreme Court, the Constitution, tax exemption for places of worship, the flag, national holidays, the two-party system, democracy, the welfare system, the present system of states, the right of immigration into the United States, the legal settlement of disputes, the national anthem, social security, the Electoral College

### Religious Sacred Cows:

The clergy, the Pope, the cross, the Ten Commandments, Religious holidays, holy places, belief in God, sacred texts

### Social Sacred Cows:

Children, weddings, marriage, the right to reproduce, motherhood, the family, doctors, the dead, funerals, burial grounds, mass public education, college education, graduation ceremonies, endangered species, historical buildings, historical statues and symbols, the goodness of rural life, man as the sexual aggressor, man as the decision maker, man as warrior, spectator sports, mobility, the automobile, progress, home ownership, egalitarianism, the right of inheritance, the right to strike, the right to choose your mate, aid to the disabled, paid vacations

Some of these sacred cows are slowly dying or are being seriously questioned while new ones are emerging and being added to the list.

Every society also has its list of taboos, or negative biases. These are people, places, ideas and things that people oppose or are generally think of as undesirable. Let's look at some of them.

### Some Taboos

Economic Taboos:

High prices, low demand for goods and services, disparity between high and low salary scales in the workplace, low salaries, depression, recession, stock market crashes, scarcity

Political Taboos:

High taxes, a police state, union of church and state, poor educational system, poor health care, pollution, slavery

Religious Taboos:

Favoritism of one religion over another by the government, immoral scenes in the mass media, desecration of sacred objects, seizure of religious properties, demands for non-discriminatory practices against women, gays, etc.

<u>Social Taboos:</u>

> Crime, substance abuse, terrorism, disloyalty, corruption, bribery, too rapid a rate of societal change, spousal abuse, child abuse, abuse of senior citizens, cruelty to animals, juvenile delinquency, suicide, scandals

What has been said about sacred cows can be said about taboos. Some are dying or are being seriously questioned while new ones are emerging.

One example of a politician using a bias from the list of sacred cows would be for him or her to stress the American value of mobility. The politician might be trying to persuade the audience to support a freeway expansion.

One example of using a bias from America's taboo list would be for a propagandist opposed to school reform to select the high tax taboo. People generally have bad feelings when the topic of high taxes is introduced.

The propagandist could stress the great expense that would be incurred by the taxpayers in any serious attempt to bring about educational reform.

**CHALLENGE TO THE EGO**

Some people need to know they've got what it takes. This challenge to the ego technique was made for them. I remember an appeal from the United States Marine Corps which said something like " you can join the Marines if you're man enough." I'm sure that the Marine Corps hoped many young men would take the bait and join up.

I once tried to use this technique on my son. I said that I didn't think he had the strength to lift up the garbage can from the garage and take it out in front of the house. This ploy only worked once as my son soon got wise to my intentions.

## FLATTERY WILL WORK WONDERS

Flattery is something people often say they don't like, but don't you believe it. If flattery isn't overdone, it can prepare an audience to better receive ideas. Flattery can defuse some angry crowds at times.

People like to be thought of as being intelligent. You can tell them they are capable of thinking for themselves and drawing their own conclusions. Of course their conclusions are based on the facts you have given them.

An audience that has been told they are needed and important to the cause will be more likely to support the ideas of the propagandist. Likewise, an audience that has been told of the sympathy that is with them for any sacrifices they have made will often be won over. Most people are hungry for recognition of any suffering they feel they have endured.

Audiences like to feel powerful. People generally like to feel that they are empowered. When they are told they are members of a winning team they will feel they are in control of events.

**EMPHASIZING CREDENTIALS**

Good credentials such as titles, degrees or awards usually impress listeners. A propagandist in speaking on an issue in American history probably would open with something like, "Since receiving my doctorate in history, I've studied American political affairs exhaustively. And I believe that…."

**TELL THEM IT'S CONFIDENTIAL**

In this technique a propagandist says what he or she is about to tell the audience is strictly confidential and privileged information. Since people generally like to think that they are "in the know" and members of the "in crowd" they are likely to accept whatever they are told. The propagandist leaks a small item from a news story or relates a new finding, hoping to win approval and support from an audience.

**STIMULATE CURIOSITY**

Whenever a propagandist can stimulate people to be curious, he or she will do it. Commercials in the mass media often include invitations to potential customers to come on down to the store and see the bargains, products or services for themselves. There is a human tendency to investigate things. Automobile dealers often encourage customers to take a test drive in any one of the new cars on the showroom floor. Publicists for cities and states often ask people to send for free brochures that loaded with colorful and interesting pictures that will hopefully attract visitors.

In a debate, a propagandist might tell his or her audience, "Would you really like to know what's behind my opponent's proposal?" The audience should be expected to show a little more interest that usual in what they're being told.

One of the debaters might suggest to the members of the audience the questions they should ask of the opponent. The opponent will then feel obligated to answer those questions. The propagandist should be sure that the questions suggested center on the weakest parts of the opposition's case.

This could put the opponent on the spot

## STRUCTURED RESPONSE

In this technique the propagandist tries to get people to respond to his or her questions with a continual stream of like answers, either positive or negative, depending on how the propagandist wants to influence the audience. The questions should be such that most people would respond in the same way. After several questions are asked the propagandist slips in the question he or she is really interested in being answered in a certain way. The propagandist hopes that habit will kick into play and that the crowd will come up with the response he or she wants.

Example:

If a politician was against gun control, he or she might ask a series of questions as follows:

Speaker: "Do you want government censorship?

Audience: "No!"

Speaker: "Do you want high taxes?"

Audience: "No!"

Speaker: "Do you want to live in a police state?"

Audience: "No!"

Speaker: "Do you want big government to keep on growing?"

Audience: "No!"

Speaker: "Do you want your sons and daughters to be sent off to war?"

Audience: "No!"

Speaker: "Do you want government gun control?"

Audience: "No!"

## IMITATE, MIMIC OR MOCK THE OPPONENT

If a propagandist attempts to put down the opposition using this technique, he or she better have some talent in the performing arts. Apparently, President Harry S. Truman did. On the eve of the presidential election of 1948, H.V. Kaltenborn, a famous radio announcer, stood by his view that Thomas E. Dewey, the Republican candidate, would defeat Truman. Kaltenborn expected a strong last minute flood of rural Republican voters would enable Dewey to pull ahead of Truman and win the White House.

The victorious Harry Truman showed no mercy to H.V. Kaltenborn. Truman publicly mocked the nation's renowned commentator, by imitating the man's facial expressions, gestures and speech to restate Kaltenborn's incorrect projection of the election results.

**AD POPULUM**

This is a device that relies in featuring whatever is current, well known or popular at the time. Simply put this technique focuses on what the propagandist thinks his or her audience wants to hear and is currently interested or concerned about.

In my classrooms at the turn of the 21$^{st}$ century, I find that most students place the Vietnam War in the category of ancient history. References to that war in any school debate would fall on deaf ears.

To effectively persuade an audience the propagandist must make his or her points relevant to the times.

**ACTION INVOLVEMENT**

If the propagandist has a chance, he or she will enlist the members of the audience in taking some action for a cause. A situation can be created in which people bond with the speaker and his or her aims. In this technique the propagandist will call on people to write letters, make telephone calls, ring doorbells, talk to friends, make financial contributions, distribute flyers and do anything to get them personally involved. The more people do for a cause, the more they'll likely support it.

**PRESENT UTOPIAN OR DYSTOPIAN FANTASIES**

A utopia literally means "no place", but generally is taken to mean an imaginary perfect society. A utopian view can paint a wonderful picture of the future in which all of our social, political, economic and environmental problems are solved.

Propagandists who project utopian concepts cater to a tendency of many people to seek perfection. We all want good outcomes from our endeavors. Many political and religious leaders have projected what they thought were perfect social orders. Hitler's Thousand Year Reich, Stalin's worker's paradise, Mussolini's forecast of the new Roman Empire, Savonarola's heavenly Florence, Napoleon's new Europe, Brigham Young's new zion in Utah – all were utopian visions.

Any politician who can stimulate his or her people to dream of a great, prosperous and problem free future is using the utopian technique on them. If a propagandist wants to research some utopian constructions of the past, he or she might examine a few of the following utopian authors and their works:

Andreae, J.V.  Christianopolis

Bacon, Francis  The New Atlantis

Bellamy, Ed  Looking Backward

Brown, J.M.  Limanora

Burton, Robert  An Utopia of Mine Own

Butler, Samuel  Erewhon

Cabet, Etienne  Voyage en Icarie

Campanella, Tommasco  City of the Sun

Chavannes, Albert  The Future Commonwealth

Chauncey, Thomas  The Crystal Button

Ellis, G. A.  New Britain

Donnelly, Ignatius  Caesar's Column

Harrington, James  Oceana

Hertzka, Dr. Theodor  Freeland

Huxley, Aldous  Brave New World

Lao-tzu  II Ching

Macrie, John  The Diothas

More, Sir Thomas  Utopia

Plato  The Republic

Skinner, B.F.  Waldon Two

Stanley, William  The Case of the Fox

Tarde, Gabriel  Underground Man

Wells, H.G.  A Modern Utopia

A dystopia is the worst imaginable society. If a person is in, let's say, a race for the presidency, he or she might try to portray a dystopia. The trick is to show how terrible the nation will be if the opponent wins the election.

If the propagandist wants to explore some dystopias, he or she might examine the following authors and their works:

Hall, Joseph  The Discovery of a New World

Orwell, George  1984

## SCARCITY SELLS

Few things attract human interest as the perception of scarcity. Scarce items usually have high value and corporate advertising makes good use of this. A real estate developer can hardly resist saying how few homes are left in his or her development.

A selective college or university seems to attract students to it. The possession or attainment of something scarce often means high prestige for the person who won the race.

## SECTION 6 – TECHNIQUES OF STYLE

**SHOCK 'EM**

A propagandist will use the shock treatment to catch his or her audience's attention.  The propagandist will make a rather outrageous, exaggerated or shocking statement as an attention getter.  There is a price to pay for using this technique.  The propagandist must have the necessary supporting data and sound reasons to back up any shocking opening remark.

I've listed a few examples of hypothetical shocking statements that might be made by partisans of some selected issues:

An Environmentalist: "The human race might not see the turn of the next century."

An Educational Reformer: "America's public schools are pretty good – for a third world nation!"

A Dietitian : "You may be killing your children."

An Opponent of Anti-ballistic missile systems: We're more likely to die from a terrorist bombing than from a missile launched from a rogue nation."

A Sociologist with a Bias Against Extreme Social Stratification:  "Karl Marx might have been right. The rich are getting richer and the poor are getting poorer."

A Scientist Concerned About Global Warming: "Pretty soon we'll have to visit our coastal cities from a sight seeing submarine."

An Ultra-feminist: "Who are the most dangerous people in the world? They're fairly easy to spot for they usually wear pants!"

A Doctor Pitted against Health Insurance Companies: "Could we win a war if our generals had to get permission to go ahead with each planned battlefield maneuver? Well doctors are facing similar circumstances today!"

One outstanding example of the shock'em technique was provided by the antics of the evangelist Aimee Semple Mc Pherson. In the late 1920s, her illustrated sermons became famous. After receiving a traffic ticket for speeding she had an idea for a sermon. One day she called out to her congregation, "Stop! You're under arrest!" Sister Aimee, as she was called, appeared on her temple platform in a police uniform, standing by a motorcycle with the sound of police siren's echoing throughout the Temple. She challenged her people to stop before they sped into hell.*

*Blumhofer, Edith   <u>Aimee Semple McPherson: Everybody's Sister</u>   William B. Eerdmans Publishing Co. Grand Rapids, Michigan 1993, pg. 261

## THE SHOTGUN APPROACH

With this technique the propagandist throws at the audience every supporting idea for his or her cause that can be thought up. The hope is that at least some of the ideas will be accepted. The more varied and heterogeneous the audience is, the better the chances to get ideas across. If the propagandist is scared to base his or her case on just one main point, this approach is a wise one.

## EMPHASIZE ONE POINT

With this technique the propagandist selects what he or she feels is the strongest argument supporting the position being taken on a subject. All other supporting arguments are excluded. It can be risky because if the opponent shoots down the propagandist's main idea the contest is over.

Abraham Lincoln debated using this approach. He was seriously opposed to slavery and in his speeches he hammered away at the problem relentlessly. The slave holding states didn't like him one bit but the free states certainly did and elected him to the presidency.

## BREAK THE ICE

The propagandist can warm up an audience to better accept the message being delivered by first telling a joke or amusing story. The audience will be more receptive to the message once their tensions are relieved.

Let's say that a speech is being given in New York City. Listeners could be told, "I almost broke my neck looking at the tops of your tall skyscrapers here." (The propagandist rubs his or her neck a little while making the remark.)

The propagandist will have amassed a collection of jokes and amusing stories appropriate to reach the groups being targeted. I've listed some topics used to break the ice.

alliteration, bathos, pathos, burlesque, caricature, conundrums, crazy acronyms, daffy definitions, irony, epigrams, hyperbole, limericks, oxymora, parody, puns, ridicule, sarcasm, sardonic remarks, satire, sick humor, synecdoche, understatement

## START COLD, GET WARM AND END HOT

I've seen motion pictures of Adolf Hitler making speeches where he used this technique to influence the crowd. He would begin calmly, like an old kindly grandfather, to slowly address his audience. Then he would begin speaking a little faster and louder and with a notable increase in enthusiasm. He would end his speech by screaming at the crowd while gesturing forcibly and using his fists to pound the podium. The crowd seemed to have accompanied the Fuehrer in his mood swings and went wild with cheers and applause.

## BUILDING THE MESSAGE AROUND A PROVERB

A proverb is a short, pithy saying that expresses a well known truth or fact in the minds of many people.

A propagandist might begin his or her speech or article with a proverb. It could be selected so as to lend support to the message being delivered. After stating the proverb, the propagandist would build a case by offering several arguments based on the proverb.

Examples of Selected Proverbs and Their Possible Uses:

Proverb:  Ambition destroys its possessor.

Possible Use:  Attacking a strong opponent in a race for political office.

Proverb:  Do good, and not ask for whom.

Possible Use:  Making a pitch for charitable donations.

Proverb:  How far that little candle throws his beams!

Possible Use:  An appeal for people to do one small deed for a cause.

Proverb:  Only the educated are free.

Possible Use:  A campaign for increased aid to education.

Proverb:  A good husband makes a good wife.  A good wife makes a good husband.

Possible Use:  Making a plea for gender equality.

Proverb:  Our fears always outnumber our dangers.

Possible Use:  A propaganda appeal in support of a risky project.

Proverb:  A little too late is much too late.

Possible use:  To criticize a town council's promised programs that were never completed.

Proverb:  When money speaks, truth keeps silent.

Possible Use:  An attack on powerful pressure groups in a state or national capital.

Proverb:  Never open the door to a little vice lest a great one enter with it.

Possible Use:  Someone speaking out against the legalization of marijuana.

## USING GESTURES AND PROPS

Humans, perhaps more than other animals, are able to show a great variety of facial expressions and body language to display emotional states and desires.

If you've ever seen many speeches, especially those given by political and religious personalities, you've undoubtedly witnessed many uses of human body parts to persuade. Who hasn't seen finger-pointing, clenched fists, chest and podium pounding, thumbs either up or down, arms akimbo and other shows of facial expression and body language?

In the 19th century, gestures in speech functioned as a code for various states of feeling projected by a speaker. In the 20th century, gesture language went out of vogue but is still with us in a less complicated form. The clever propagandist will often practice expressions of the face and body attempting to win the response he or she wants from the audience.

Props are stage properties used in show business. The art of propaganda resembles dramatic art in some ways. Increasingly, public opinion is shaped by more than words alone. Image making is the rage today and props are necessary to this enterprise. Some often seen props are listed as follows:

insignias: flags, medals, ribbons, hats, uniforms, logos, badges of authority, etc.

large picture backdrops

books: used as a backdrop to make the speaker seem scholarly and wise

charts and graphs

music

sound effects

mood lighting

video screens tied to the internet

## MAKING A STATEMENT THAT DOESN'T FACE REBUTTAL

In a typical traditional form of debate, there are usually two speakers on each side of a proposition. Two speakers are for the proposition (the affirmative side) and two speakers are against the proposition (the negative side).

Each speaker delivers both a constructive speech and a rebuttal speech. A constructive speech presents facts and evidence for or against a proposition, while a rebuttal speech answers the arguments and evidence of the opposing speakers.

In this traditional debate form the speaking order is:

Constructive speeches (eight minutes each)

1.  First affirmative

2.  First negative

3.  Second affirmative

4.  Second negative

Rebuttal speeches (four minutes each)

1.  First negative

2.  First affirmative

3.  Second negative

4.  Second affirmative

The rebuttal speech of the second affirmative provides the speaker an opportunity to make a strong statement, perhaps a catchy slogan, which will not leave time for any rebuttal.

## MAKING A PRE-EMPTIVE STRIKE

A propagandist attacks his or her opposition on the point that is central to their case before they the opposition opens their mouths. In this technique the first affirmative debater challenges or answers the opposition's strongest argument. In this way it's possible to defuse the thrust of the opponent's attack.

There is danger in doing this maneuver. If the debater makes a miscalculation about his or her opponent's chief argument it could mean trouble.

## SECTION 7 – TECHNIQUES OF REASON AND COMMON SENSE

**USING THE SOCRATIC METHOD**

Socrates (469 B.C.- 399 B.C.) is the famous Greek philosopher who developed what is now called the Socratic Method.

This technique works well with two or a few people in a philosophical conversation. It is assumed the terms being used in the discussion are well understood and have clear definitions accepted by all the participants. As the discussion progresses, it becomes apparent, through careful questioning, that the definitions of terms differed or had minor flaws. It would then become apparent that true knowledge of an issue or problem being discussed was inadequate to reach a sound conclusion. As more time passes, the definitions of terms would improve becoming more universal and applicable to all examples.

No satisfactory conclusion might be reached, but the goal of finding true and universal definitions would be furthered.

In the Socratic Method, ignorance must be acknowledged, to do otherwise is to take a "know-it-all position.

Propagandists can use the Socratic way of arguing with someone who brings up ideas such as there should be a drug free America, family values must be upheld, Caucasians are a superior race or males should dominate females. In each of these statements, definitions would be carefully examined through extensive questioning. The discussion leader could start by asking questions such as "What is a drug?", "What are family values?," "What is a Caucasian?", "What does it mean to be superior?" "What is a male and a female?" and "What does it mean to dominate?"

This technique is designed to break apart vague definitions used by opponents. If the propagandist is lucky, he or she may put the opposition on the ropes if they haven't done their homework on the terms they use. The opponents may try several countermeasures. One might be to use a non-sequitur and another might be to answer the question with another question. The skilled propagandist always tries to prepare for his or her opponent's countermeasures.

## USE METAPHORS AND SIMILES

The use of figures of speech helps to leave main ideas in the minds of an audience. Of all the figures of speech used by propagandists, I have noticed that metaphors and similes seem to head the list.

A metaphor is a figure of speech in which a term is transferred from the object it ordinarily designates to an object it may designate only by implicit comparison or analogy.

Examples:

| Metaphors | Literal Meanings |
| --- | --- |
| Evening of life | last years |
| Slime bucket with legs | a truly terrible person |
| A watermelon | a fat person |
| Catcher's mitts | large hands |

A simile is a figure of speech in which two essentially unlike things are compared and typically uses the words "like" or "as".

Examples:

That symphony orchestra sounds like a thousand meowing cats all out of tune.

She's as nutty as the topping on a chocolate sundae.

The new dog was running around the yard like a balloon that suddenly lost all of its air.

One good example of the use of similes is the acceptance speech made by George Herbert Walker Bush at the Republican National Convention in New Orleans on August 18, 1988. He said, "We are a nation of communities, of tens and tens of thousands of ethnic, religious, social, business, labor union, neighborhood, regional and other organizations, all of them varied, voluntary and unique…a brilliant diversity spread like stars, like a thousand points of light in a broad and peaceful sky."

## TURN A PROBLEM INTO AN OPPORTUNITY

In public speaking the propagandist often has to deal with hecklers and usually is prepared for this kind of situation. When heckling started at a speech being delivered by a prominent candidate for the presidency, he responded "One great thing about our country is that people here have the freedom to speak their minds."

Sample Responses to Hecklers:

A name-calling heckler: "In words that I learned in the playground, sticks and stones will break my bones but names will never hurt me."

Accusations of wrong doing: "Let he who is without sin cast the first stone."

Embarrassing question: "I won't dignify that question with an answer."

Foul language: "Your dear mother would be ashamed of your behavior tonight!"

Sarcastic remark: "Hey buddy or lassie, you're sharp as a drill and twice as boring!"

## HELP FROM GIANTS OF THE PAST AND PRESENT

A politician raging against his or her opponent who holds high office might quote the famous statement made by Lord Aston, "All power corrupts, and absolute power corrupts absolutely."

A propagandist using quotations can come off as a person who is educated, scholarly and wise when well selected quotations are used appropriately.

## TURN A WEAKNESS INTO A STRENGTH

Propagandists who have sinned or done something wrong, claim they've been reborn as a more effective people.

A political party not anticipating a particular problem, say they don't waste time planning for things before they happen, but remain flexible and ready to meet any problem.

A group of students criticized for having mediocre grades, say that being well-rounded and not specialized in academics, has been a blessing. They are better prepared for life outside of the ivory tower.

## CHOOSE WORDS WISELY

Propagandists tailor their vocabulary to suit their target audiences. Foreign words and phrases are avoided unless the audience is a group of scholarly folks. If propagandist's choices of words makes them incomprehensible to their listeners, they'll usually lose them.

## YES, BUT...

Occasional conspicuous candor can help build a propagandist's long range credibility. Josef Goebbels, Nazi Germany's propaganda chief, practiced candor on the German people. He said yes, we are losing the war, but secret weapons being developed will turn things around. Because of his seeming honesty, many people in Nazi Germany believed him.

When Vice President Richard Nixon traveled to the Soviet Union in July 1959 to open an American exhibit in Moscow, many Russians put the representatives of America on the spot.

American attendants were asked some rather tough questions. Russians wanted to know why African Americans were oppressed. It isn't wise for a propagandist to directly contradict his or her audience and the American attendants knew that. Their response was a "Yes, But..." way of handling the question. They acknowledged that it was a serious domestic problem, but that we were trying to make a more just situation. This response, according to observers, seemed to make the Russians more receptive to what we had to say on other issues.

## EXERCISES FOR SECTION 1

Practice in using the techniques of Section 1:

SIMPLIFICATION

Write a simplified summary of the American Declaration of Independence.

Write an easy to understand explanation of what a customer should look for in purchasing an automobile.

CONCURRENCY

Choose any policy, person, product or thing you <u>oppose</u> and try to link it with negative associations. (Hint: If you would oppose the use of alcoholic beverages, link that use with a concurrent increase in highway fatalities and violent crimes.)

Choose any policy, person, product or thing you <u>support</u> and try to link it with positive associations. (Hint: If you would support NASA, try to link the agency with other fields in which are simultaneously advancing our body of knowledge.)

POST HOC

Choose a politician or policy that you <u>support</u> and try to establish a series of positive effects that flowed from the actions of the politician or the enforcement of the policy.

Choose a politician or policy that you <u>oppose</u> and try to establish a series of negative effects that flowed from the actions of the politician or the enforcement of the policy.

## GENERALIZATION

Use several generalizations in a <u>negative</u> descriptive paragraph of any person, place or thing of your choice.

Use several generalizations in a <u>positive</u> descriptive paragraph of any person, place or thing of your choice.

## FAULTY ANALOGY

Make a claim that going to school is analogous to going to work. Present reasons to support your analogy. In a separate paragraph, show why your analogy is faulty.

Claim that the carrying out of capital punishment by a state government is analogous to the killing of cattle in a slaughterhouse. Present reasons to support your analogy. In a separate paragraph, show why your analogy is faulty.

## CONDEMNING THE ORIGIN

Write a xenophobic (fear or hatred of foreigners) article in which you condemn something because of its foreign origin. (Hint: You could condemn the use of high school exit examinations because of a French origin or you could deplore the use of foreign words and expressions in our American language usage.)

## FALSE CONVERSION OF PROPOSITIONS

Write a political statement followed by an assertion that does not follow. (Hint: You could say that Republicans and Democrats are truly patriotic Americans and then go on to state that all true Americans are either Republicans or Democrats.)

## WHAT IS TRUE OF THE PARTS IS TRUE FOR THE WHOLE

Write a paragraph in support of a politician of your choice claiming that his or her good points are indicative of his or her general character.

## THE BLACK AND WHITE FALLACY

Write a paragraph in support of a proposed amendment to the United States Constitution using the black and white fallacy. (Hint: You could claim that those who oppose the removal of the Electoral College system from the Constitution are undemocratic while those who support it are democratic.)

## USING AN ILLICIT DEFINITION

Choose any of the following words and write an example of how the definition of the word can be altered, twisted and/or made to be misleading:

Word List: democracy, depression, pornography, sexual harassment. (Hint: Use the word communism to cover all socialist systems of government in the world.)

## FALLACY OF BIASED SAMPLING

Choose a subject for polling. Solicit responses to your questions from at least fifteen people of the same sex, approximate age and occupation as you. Tabulate the results. Then ask at least fifteen people of the opposite sex, age and occupation as your own. Tabulate the results. Do you find great differences in your results? Explain.

## THE GAMBLER'S FALLACY

Write a paragraph using this fallacy to encourage people to play a lottery game or write a paragraph as if you were a stockbroker in which role you encourage customers to buy a stock plagued by a poor performance record.

## THE FALLACY OF INCONSISTENCY

Choose any topic and write about it using inconsistent premises. (Hint: A graduation speaker says that all graduates should go to college or vocational schools to prepare for a career. The speaker then appeals to the girls in the class to get married, have children and stay home to raise them.)

## APPEAL TO INAPPROPRIATE AUTHORITY

Write an advertisement using this technique for any product, to support a political candidate, or to advocate a cause or policy of your choice.

## SECTION REVIEW PAPER

Write a propaganda paper for a politician, product or cause of your choice in which you use at least three of the techniques from the exercises in section 1. At the end of your paper, write the names of the techniques you have selected to use in your writing.

## BUILDING VOCABULARY

Define the following words used in section 1 and use each of them in a sentence.

<u>Word List:</u> logic, concurrency, post hoc, correspondence, proposition, polarized, illicit, invalid

## EXERCISES FOR SECTION 2

Practice in using the techniques of Section 2:

USE OF AMBIGUOUS WORDS

Use ambiguous words in writing an appeal to high school students to go to an imaginary or actual college or university. Underline the ambiguous words that you have used in your appeal. (Words such as good, superior, comprehensive, friendly, progressive, innovative, prestigious, highly rated, exciting, and multi-cultural are often used in publicity messages for colleges and universities.)

AD HOMINEM

This is your chance to go primitive in letting off steam. Choose any person, place or thing and go on a verbal attack with words as barbed weapons.

BEGGING THE QUESTION

Make three unproven statements, as though they were fact, in support of any person, place or thing of your choice. After this, make three unproven statements, as though they were fact, in opposition to any person, place or thing of your choice.

THE WICKED ALTERNATIVE

Support any person, place or thing of your choice by pointing to its wicked alternative. (Hint: I know Dad has a serious disease but it's better than a coffin.)

NON-SEQUITUR

List any three questions you feel would be a challenge to a person being questioned. Answer each question using the non-sequitur technique. Whatever you do, don't in any way really answer the question, just seem to be answering the question.

ACCUSING THE ACCUSER

Write three accusative statements aimed at an imaginary opponent. Have the imaginary opponent make a counter accusation in response to each accusative statement. *Hint: Older Brother, "You didn't eat your spinach! Younger Brother, "Yeah! You didn't eat your carrots!")

NAME CALLING

Research newspapers, magazines, radio and television broadcasts, the Internet and books looking for good examples of name-calling. In your study indicate your feelings about your findings.

THE USE OF SATIRE

Write a satire of one of the following practices or behaviors in American society.

Over consumption of natural resources, continuing growth of suburbia, the drive to build the tallest skyscraper, our love affair with the automobile, the craving for fast food, gender discrimination, the shopping mall as a social center, the inundation of sexual images in the mass media, the rise in the influence of corporate power over many aspects of life, the amount of time spent before a computer, the high salaries paid to top athletes, the gun culture, the drug culture, the endangered health care system, the escape into virtual reality

## REPARTEE

Write an imaginary exchange of sarcastic words between two actual or imaginary characters. Make the exchange of words as sharp and witty as you can. Pretend that the two adversaries are engaged in a verbal archery contest. Share your example with the class.

## CHOOSE A SCAPEGOAT

Write down at least two scapegoats for each problem in the following word list:

The failure of the American involvement in Vietnam.

Women's under representation in the seats of political, academic, business and religious power in America.

The persistence of homelessness in America.

The poor performance of American youth in international competitive examinations in science and mathematics.

America's high divorce rate.

Gridlock on America's roadways.

## SECTION REVIEW PAPER

Write a propaganda paper for a politician, product or cause of your choice in which you use at least three of the techniques in this section. At the end of your writing, list the names of the techniques that you have chosen to use.

## VOCABULARY BUILDING

Define the following terms used in section 2 and use each term in a sentence: ambiguous, ad hominem, preemptive, non-sequitur, gutter snipe, boondocks, bizarre, "rube goldberg", satire, repartee, scapegoat, Ku Klux Klan

# EXERCISES FOR SECTION 3

Practice in using the techniques of Section 3:

## APPEAL TO TRADITION

Use this appeal to write in support of any cause of your choice. After this, write another appeal in opposition to any cause of your choice.

## DEMAND FOR SPECIAL CONSIDERATION

Write a propaganda paper in support of an affirmative action policy in college and university admissions for the minority group of your choice.

## APPEAL TO THE EMOTIONS

Make a written emotional appeal for any political, economic or social cause of your choice. Indicate the emotions you selected for your propaganda paper at the end of your writing.

## PERSONIFICATION

Write a paragraph supporting a cause of your choice in which you use the personification technique. After this, write a paragraph attacking a cause of your choice using this technique.

## THE USE OF HOT AND COLD WORDS

Expand the listing of offensive terms and their euphemisms that are found in the text under the heading of this technique. Your list should show at least ten items.

## LOOK TO THE FUTURE AND BE OPTIMISTIC

Write an optimistic propaganda paper in support of any issue in the following list or, if you wish, write on an issue of your own choosing.

Issue List: the drive for gender equality, race and ethnic relations, ways of controlling violence, space exploration, the future of medical care, the future of education, how to end wars in the world, globalism

## LET ALTRUISM REIGN

Write a propaganda paper in support of a philanthropic activity, foundation or organization of your choice. Think of some innovative fund raising techniques.

## SECTION REVIEW

Write a propaganda paper for a politician, product or cause of your choice in which you use at least three of the techniques in this section. At the end of your writing, list the names of the techniques that you have chosen to use.

## EXERCISES FOR SECTION 4

Practice in using the techniques of Section 4:

### QUOTING OUT OF CONTEXT

Write a quotation out of context. You should research motion picture reviews, political speeches, book reviews, magazine and newspaper articles to obtain original material for your assignment. Write the selected original material and then write a quotation out of context. Put three dot journalism (three dots signify that words have been omitted) to work to distort the meaning that was originally intended by the author or speaker whose statements you are using. Share your work in class.

### USE OF NUMBERS TO IMPRESS

Write a propaganda paper publicizing a city, state or nation of your choice in which you list all the superlatives you can find that can be expressed numerically.

Things you might investigate: the number of schools, places of worship, public buildings, parks, playgrounds, growth figures, famous sons and daughters, the number of years since founding, per capita income, life expectancy, annual imports and exports, literacy rate, railway and road mileage, the number of radios, telephones, automobiles, television sets, anything that's big or tall

## FALSE DILEMMA

For each of the incomplete dilemmas listed in this exercise supply at least three possible words to complete them:

Example: Elect Cranston for president or face (ruin, four worrisome years, the prospect of a do nothing government).

Fight for your country or_____

Widen the highway or_____

Prepare for war or _____

What will make the statements false dilemmas is to offer only one option when in fact there are more.

## USING A MINOR POINT TO DISCREDIT A PERSON, PLACE OR THING

Use a minor point in a paragraph to discredit any person, place or thing of your choice.

## LEADING QUESTION

Make up a list of five leading questions you might ask of a person of your choice in an imaginary interview. Be sure that your questions are structured in such a way that they can only be answered with either a yes or no response. Also make sure that regardless of how your questions are answered, the person answering them will be compromised.

SEEK SIMPLE ANSWERS

Choose a politician, product or cause of your choice and write a propaganda paper in which you ask one or more questions designed to illicit a simple answer from your listening or reading audience.

EXAGGERATION OF CONSEQUENCES

Write a propaganda paper that exaggerates the consequences of the passage of a law that you favor. Put a positive spin into your writing. Then, write another propaganda paper that exaggerates the consequences of the passing of a law that you oppose. Put a negative spin into your writing.

DOUBLE TALK

Use double talk in writing a propaganda paper advocating two inconsistent policies at odds with each other.

Possible topics (You may use any of these listed topics or use one of your own choosing.):

Let's keep dangerous substances under control but we must continue to subsidize tobacco growing.

Let's reduce senseless crimes of violence but let's not be too restrictive about the sale of guns.

We need an expanding economy but we must curb growth.

Citizens who are eighteen years old are welcomed into the armed forces and have the right to vote but they must not be allowed to consume alcoholic beverages.

We should spend more on social welfare programs and push forward on my tax cutting proposal.

## MANIPULATING NUMBERS

Make a search of the mass media looking for examples of manipulating numbers. Share your findings in class.

## BIG LIE

Use the big lie technique to discredit any person, place or thing of your choice. Try searching the mass media for examples of big lies.

## PLACEMENT OF EMPHASIS

Use this technique in writing two propaganda papers – one positive and the other negative. For example you could refer to television set ownership in Brazil (year 2000 figures) that 34 million Brazilians have television sets. You could also say that 131 million Brazilians don't have television sets.

You may choose a topic from the following topic list:

Airline safety, health insurance in the United States, indoor plumbing in any nation, the number who drowned in the Titanic disaster, % of casualties in the armed forces of the United States in World War II

## INNUENDO

Use innuendo in making damaging statements about one topic you'll choose from the following categories:

World leaders, nations of the world, cities of the world, entertainers, music forms, careers. Example: "The city is playing classical music in the town square to get teenagers to vacate the area." The underlying message is that teenagers don't like classical music.

## APPEAL TO IGNORANCE

Use this appeal in a propaganda paper attacking the content of any of the programming you select from the mass media.

## CARD STACKING

Use card stacking to support any political, economic or social policy, manufactured product or service of your choice in a paragraph. Then use the technique to attack any political, economic or social policy, manufactured product or service of your choice in another paragraph.

## STRESS HIGH MORAL PRINCIPLES

Use this technique to support any politician, policy, product or service of your choice.

## FALSE URGENCY

Search the mass media for examples illustrating this technique and share your findings in class.

## PRAISE ONE THING THE OPPONENT HAS DONE, THEN ON TO THE ATTACK

Use this technique to attack any world leader of your choice. The aim is to seem somewhat fair and balanced in your overall negative assessment of your targeted victim.

## MAKE A MINOR CONFESSION AND SAY THAT NOW YOU'VE SEEN THE LIGHT

Choose any one of the following topics in writing an appeal for people to stop the behavior you once might have done yourself:

Topics: excessive drinking of alcoholic beverages, use of curse words, excessive speeding in a car, running red lights, use of illegal drugs, cutting classes in school, being cruel to animals, exhibiting violent behavior, having unprotected sexual relations, vandalizing property

## SET UP A STRAW MAN

Use the straw man technique in a propaganda paper opposing any one of the following activities or one of your own choosing:

Activities: building fossil fuel power plants, building vehicles that consume large amounts of fossil fuels, drilling for oil off the coasts of America, American policing of world trouble spots, America's dependence on private transportation; America's stress on building single family housing, the construction of nuclear power plants

## TELLING THEM YOU WERE GOING TO LIE BUT COULDN'T DO IT

Use this technique in an imaginary speech on any one of the following subjects or one of your own choosing:

A principal's speech on the future of education presented at a parent-teacher meeting.

A speech to high school students interested in becoming professional athletes.

A speech to medical personnel at a local hospital.

A commercial for any product or service you want to promote.

## BUILD A POTEMKIN VILLAGE

Search any real estate advertisements of new developments (in undesirable or inconvenient locations) for signs of "Potemkin villages". Share your findings in class.

Search travel magazines for articles about places that use "Potemkin villages"to present a false impression either cities or countries around the world that want to encourage tourism.

# MAKE THE IDEAS BEING SUPPORTED OR OPPOSED SEEM TO BE FORGONE CONCLUSIONS

Use this technique in writing a propaganda paper about a politician or policy of your choice.

## DEFINE TERMS TO SUIT GOALS

Use this technique in writing a promotional advertisement for a resort hotel. (Hint: Define exciting getaway in terms that suit your goals.)

## SECTION REVIEW PAPER

Write a propaganda paper for a politician, product or cause in which you use at least three of the techniques from this section. At the end of your writing, list the names of the techniques that you have chosen.

## VOCABULARY BUILDING

Define the following terms used in section 4 and use each term in a sentence.

Terms: context, dilemma, innuendo, straw man, Potemkin village, double-talk.

# EXERCISES FOR SECTION 5

Practice in using the techniques of Section 5:

## APPEAL TO AUTHORITY

Use this technique in writing three statements about each of the following subjects:

Causes you support

Causes you oppose

Products or services you favor

Products or services you don't favor

## REPITITION

Choose a product or service you favor and write an advertisement about it using this technique.

## USE SLOGANS

Write a slogan of your own making for each of the following subjects:

A candidate for President

A fund raiser for AIDS

A product of your choice

A service of your choice

## BANDWAGON

Use this technique in a paragraph in support of a project you'd like to see built in your community, state or nation.

## PLAIN FOLKS

Write a public relations paper to make scientists and technicians working for NASA seem like regular fellows and gals.

## TRANSFER

Write an advertisement using this technique to encourage young people to use a product or service of your choice.

## TESTIMONIAL

Make a list of people you'd use in making testimonial appeals for each of the following products and services. Briefly explain the reasons for your selections in each case.

Products and services:

stereo systems

new computers

women's shoes

golf clubs

cruise ship vacations

cosmetic materials

an HMO

dance lessons

## USING A BIAS

Write a promotional paper encouraging people to seek the services of an investment company of your choice.

## CHALLENGE TO THE EGO

A college or university of your choice wants to increase student enrollment. Use this technique in a promotional paper to catch the attention of high school students.

## FLATTERY WILL WORK WONDERS

Use flattery in a propaganda appeal to potential donors to a charity of your choice.

## EMPHASIZING CREDENTIALS

Pretend that you are running for the office of student body president at a high school or college. If you don't have any credentials you should make up a few to impress your audience.

## TELL THEM IT'S CONFIDENTIAL

Put yourself in the place of a high school math teacher addressing students on the first day of class. You'll tell them confidentially what plans are being discussed for future changes in the curriculum that might affect them. Pledge them to be secretive about this information. If you prefer to be a teacher of another subject other than math, go right ahead.

## STIMULATE CURIOSITY

Think of yourself as an alternative energy advocate trying to get people to switch from fossil fuel use to renewable energy sources. Try to get your audience curious about your cause in a one paragraph appeal.

## STRUCTURED RESPONSE

Use this technique to persuade people to use any product or service of your choice.

## IMITATE, MIMIC OR MOCK THE OPPONENT

Choose any leader of what the United States government describes as a "rogue state" and mock him or her in a paragraph or two.

## AD POPULUM

Imagine that you are a speaker going to high schools to inform students about the need to develop safe driving habits. Use popular and current references to connect with your audiences. In other words, play to the gallery!

## ACTION INVOLVEMENT

Imagine that you are a high school principal faced with a school that is littered with refuse and graffiti and showing the effects of vandalism. Try to get your student body involved in solving these problems in a speech calling for action.

## PRESENT UTOPIAN OR DYSTOPIAN FANTASIES

Imagine yourself as a stockbroker and write a technological utopian fantasy encouraging investors to put their money into a new biotechnology offering.


## SCARCITY SELLS

Use this technique in writing an advertisement for any product or service of your choice.


## SECTION REVIEW PAPER

Write a propaganda paper for a politician, product, service or cause of your choice in which you use at least three techniques from this section. At the end of your paper, write the names of the techniques that you have used.


## BUILDING VOCABULARY

Define the following terms used in section 5 and use each one in a sentence.


Word List: slogan, testimonial, bias, sacred cow, taboo, ego, utopia, dystopia

*Henry T. Conserva*

# EXERCISES FOR SECTION 6

Practice in using the techniques of Section 6

SHOCK 'EM

Write just the opening shocking statement of a speech on each of the following topics:

Our Declining Pool of Natural Resources

The World's Population Problem

Marriage Is an Endangered Institution

Plagues Are Coming

Atomic Weapons Are Proliferating

The Scourge of Aids

America's Infrastructure Crisis

The Outlook for World Peace in This Century

THE SHOTGUN APPROACH

For each of the following debate resolutions, list at least five affirmative and five negative arguments:

Resolved: That the Constitution of the United States be amended to allow prayers to be said in public schools.

Resolved: That the Constitution of the United States be amended to make the burning of the American flag a criminal offense.

Resolved: That the voting age be lowered to 16 in federal elections.

Resolved: That capital punishment be prohibited in the United States.

## EMPHASIZE ONE POINT

For each of the following debate resolutions, provide what you feel is the strongest affirmative argument and the strongest negative argument:

Resolved: That a national system of medical care for all citizens be established in the United States.

Resolved: That the Electoral College be abolished.

Resolved: That the use of illegal drugs be decriminalized.

Resolved: That English be made the official language of the United States.

## BREAK THE ICE

Write at least three jokes or amusing stories that would be good icebreakers to warm up an audience and relieve tensions.

## START COLD, GET WARM AND END HOT

Imagine that you are an environmentalist trying to get support for saving the whales. Write a short speech by starting with some simple statements without much emotion then gradually increase the number of emotional statements ending in a crescendo of emotional statements

## BUILDING THE MESSAGE AROUND A PROVERB

Choose one cause you support and one cause you oppose. Search out and list what you feel would be appropriate proverbs to build your message around for each of the causes you have selected.

## USING GESTURES AND PROPS

For each of the following speeches, list your choices of the props you feel would be most effective and in each case explain why you chose the props you did:

A presidential speech to the American people calling on them to support an increase in military spending.

A televised promotional message supporting the purchase of life insurance.

A televised promotional message on any product or service of your choice.

A televised speech to young people on the dangers of drug use.

MAKING A STATEMENT THAT DOESN'T FACE REBUTTAL

Imagine that you are the second affirmative speaker making a rebuttal speech. For each of the following debate resolutions supply a strong, catchy statement that will not leave time for any rebuttal:

Resolved: That the voting age be lowered to sixteen.

Resolved: That the Electoral College be abolished.

Resolved: That an equal rights amendment to the Constitution of the United States be adopted.

Resolved: (any resolution of your choice)

MAKING A PRE-EMPTIVE STRIKE

In each of the following debate resolutions, take the position of the first affirmative speaker in the debate and attack what you feel to be the strongest argument of the negative team:

Resolved: That all drivers of automobiles and trucks be required to wear crash helmets.

Resolved: That women be allowed to serve in combat positions in the armed forces of the United States.

Resolved: That no generating plants powered by nuclear reactors be built in the United States.

Resolved: (any resolution of your choice)

## SECTION REVIEW PAPER

Write a propaganda paper for a politician, product or service of your choice in which you use at least three techniques from this section. At the end of your paper, write the names of the techniques you have used.

## BUILDING VOCABULARY

Define the following terms used in section 6 and use each term in a sentence:

Word List: Shock, affirmative, resolution (debate). joke, crescendo, emotionalism, proverb, rebut

## EXERCISES FOR SECTION 7

Practice in using the techniques of Section 7

USING THE SOCRATIC METHOD

Students should work in pairs to discuss a controversial problem of the day. The discussion should focus on the definitions of key terms that are important to the understanding of the issues involved in the problem. A considerable amount of time should be spent on reaching agreement on definitions even though no overall resolution of the problem may occur.

USE METAPHORS AND SIMILES

Write an appeal in support of a cause of your choice or write a promotional message for any product or service in which you use at least two metaphors or similes. Underline these figures of speech and identify them with a letter <u>M</u> for metaphor or with a letter <u>S</u> for simile upon completion of your work.

TURN A PROBLEM INTO AN OPPORTUNITY

List five problem situations of your choice. In each case write what you feel would be an appropriate response that would turn the problem into an opportunity to defuse it.

## HELP FROM GIANTS OF THE PAST AND PRESENT

Choose a cause, product, service and person you'd like to support. For each of these subjects search out a quotation from a famous person, past or present, that would be effective in a promotional message for each subject.

## TURN A WEAKNESS INTO A STRENGTH

For each of the following hypothetical situations try to turn the weakness into a strength for the person under siege:

A European journalist asks an American high school principal why American students score so low in international science and mathematics examinations. What does the principal say in defense of American secondary education?

A political reporter questions a politician's ability to command given the close election the official barely won. What response does the politician make?

An environmentalist in a discussion with a Detroit automobile executive demands to know why his company continues to produce gas guzzling cars, trucks and vans. How does the executive handle this accusation?

## CHOOSE WORDS WISELY

Write two promotional messages for any politician, product, service or cause of your choice. In one message you'll use complex, difficult, obscure or even foreign terms. In the second message you'll rewrite the first message substituting simpler and less obscure terms.

YES, BUT...

Reply to the following statements with a "yes, but..." response:

"Isn't it true that men earn more money than women doing the same work?"

"I hear that you Americans consume more energy than any other people in the world."

I understand that Americans refuse to use the metric system."

SECTION REVIEW PAPER

Write a propaganda paper for a politician, product or cause of your choice in which you use at least three techniques from this section. At the end of your paper, write the names of the techniques you have used.

BUILDING VOCABULARY

Define the following terms used in section 7 and use each one in a sentence:

Word List: Socratic method, metaphor, simile, definition, countermeasure, heckler

## About the Author

Henry T. Conserva has taught in public secondary schools in the San Francisco Bay Area of California for over fifty years. In his position as a debating coach, he was involved in developing critical thinking skills among his students. He thought knowledge of propaganda techniques was essential in arming his students against the many questionable arguments they often faced in their debates. He noted that many of the students became skeptical consumers as they saw through many of the advertising appeals that were aimed at them on a daily basis. His hope has always been that all students would benefit from knowing at least some of the ways used by those who wish to brainwash them.

Printed in the United States
22126LVS00002B/235-242

9 781410 704962